Montessori
in the HOME

A preliminary study and practical application of the principles and method of Dr. Maria Montessori for the use of parents in the home

Cover design and art work by Louis Ricucci

Copyright © 1963 Jerome Study Group

Dear Reader,

As the publisher of this second edition I would like to tell you something about the two women who figured so prominently in the final presentation of a booklet many parents have requested.

The first is readily recognized. Her name is in the title. An understanding of her approach to the development of the child and how it could apply to parents in the home is the raison d'être of the second woman's distinction.

Maria Montessori was an Italian physician and educator who worked in the first half of the present century. She was the first woman to receive the Degree of Doctor of Medicine from the University of Rome Medical School, where she did post-graduate work in the Psychiatric Clinic, and was appointed in 1899 Directress of the State Orthophrenic School. It was there she formulated the educational theories which she was later to develop into the philosophy of the child commonly referred to as the Montessori Method. Its revolutionary approach to the concept of man earned her the right to be ranked with Sigmund Freud and John Dewey.

Montessori wished to ensure for every child a life as deep, as rich, as complete as possible. Precisely the same wish, not only for her own nine children, but for all children, led Mrs. John O'Keefe of Chevy Chase, Maryland to form the group whose two years' study and work finds its culmination in this pamphlet. Mrs. O'Keefe was responsible for the inception, direction and completion of the work. Without "Martha," as she will be forever immemorialized in the hearts of many a local "Montessori" mother, none of this would have been possible. But for her abundant good sense, her dedication, her persistence and her courage, the fruits of the work would have been far less nourishing to the children. Certainly, without her wit and grace, it would have been far less enjoyable for their mothers.

The two sections of the pamphlet each represent one year's work, Part I having been published separately at the end of the first year. Part II is intended to explicate the application of the principles enunciated in the first section.

Special thanks are due to Vincent Brown for his invaluable assistance in the initial preparation of the pamphlet for publication and to Robert Rice & Paul Ruddell for their many hours of consultation before the printing of this second edition. And this publisher wishes to express her gratitude to all the mothers, fathers, and children who participated in this study and who continue to do so by trying to find a greater depth of meaning in the relationship between parent and child.

—*a. f. b.*

CONTENTS

PREFACE iii

INTRODUCTION 1

PART I. A PRELIMINARY STUDY

    The Work of the Child.................................... 5
    The Work of the Parent.................................. 9
    "Human Dignity is Born of the Sentiment of One's
      Independence"...................................... 13
    Education of the Senses and Movement: The Basis of the
      Montessori Method 15
    From Six to Twelve..................................... 16
    Comments 19

PART II. PRACTICAL APPLICATION

    Writing and Reading..................................... 20
    Science 24
    Measure and Number................................... 26
    History 32
    Art 34
    The Use of the Didactic Material........................ 36
    Foreign Language 42
    Some Personal Experiences.............................. 43
    Comments 46
    Bibliography 48

MONTESSORI IN THE HOME

INTRODUCTION

One need only peruse the recent literature on child development to see the unanimous agreement regarding the importance of the first six years of a child's life. The other important word that is seen repeatedly is "parent." There can be little disagreement about the immense influence parents exert during the formative years—the pre-school years—the time when a child's adult-world consists mainly of his mother and father.

Parents have been criticized for trying to make the most fruitful these extremely important early years. Such terms as "pushiness," "pressure," "over-intellectual stress" have been hurled at parents; unfortunately, in many cases this is rightly so. However, parents in Montessori groups, such as the one which gave birth to this pamphlet, are quite aware of the necessity of following the child's lead—without pushing or pressuring him. Montessori's own discussion of sensitive periods would, in itself, preclude the presenting of materials too early.

The following chapters document the fact that parents are capable of providing a healthy, stimulating atmosphere in which children can grow physically, emotionally, and intellectually; they demonstrate that this is the parents' natural responsibility. The present pamphlet should also bolster the confidence of those who are sincerely interested in child development—their own child's development. Further, it will provide a more organized approach for parents to implement, rather than the trial-and-error system which leads to much uncertainty for both child and parent.

The possible misuse or misinterpretation of the Montessori method is the most frequently voiced criticism made of efforts to bring this educational approach into the home. One need only realize, however, that parents will find other approaches if this one is denied to them. Moreover, the availability of a systematized philosophy of childhood education is a necessity during the years when the parents serve as the only educators of their children.

The suggestions in this pamphlet are not seen as a substitute for later, more formal education. Rather, they are viewed as the means for nurturing the intellectual seed which will later blossom in the grown adult. Thus this endeavor should present to schools individuals eager to continue the learning already begun at home, and possessed of a very positive attitude toward work, study, and play.

However, even after a child enters nursery school or kindergarten there is no lessening in the importance of the parents' role in the education of the child. A general dissatisfaction with many of the current educational policies is widespread. Educators and parents have voiced their concerns about "lock-step" progression through the elementary grades, and about the underestimation of children's capacities to learn. In a recent *New York Times Magazine* (28 April 1963) article entitled "Little Brains Think Big," Vivian Cadden expressed the thesis that today's youngsters have an astonishing amount of information, although parents and educators are still inclined to think of them as "cute little tykes" who are capable of educational busywork, at most. Citing Dr. Jerome S. Bruner, professor of psychology at Harvard University, the article quotes his statement: "The foundations of any subject may be taught to anybody at any age in some form." As a way of illustrating the gap between today's pupils and the outmoded curricula, and also depicting the boredom and wasting of precious years that occurs in the elementary grades, the following story is related:

> Two little kindergarten boys were standing in a school yard during recess. Two jets zoomed by overhead. The boys looked up.
> "707," said the first boy.
> The other nodded and pointed at the second plane. "DC 6," he said.
> The boys then proceeded to discuss the comparative cruising speeds of the two planes, the displacement of the jet engines, the two hydraulic systems and the relative fuel consumption. They had just launched into a comparison of the dyhedral of the wings when the school bell rang.
> "Well," said one boy to the other with a sigh, "we might as well go back in and string some more of those damn beads."

The home can no longer be viewed as a place where only a child's physical needs are met. Recent writings on child development have emphasized the necessity of meeting emotional needs. To this we add the next most obvious need to be met—the intellectual. Since children seem capable, and want to learn at a much earlier age than formerly recognized, it seems only natural that aid in this area be given to parents.

Maria Montessori's ideas about children and the methods she evolved through careful observation, seem to provide many of the sought-after answers. In addition, the parent is a highly important factor in the educational equation. What he does, the attitudes he holds, his basic concept of his role, all influence to a marked degree, a child's development and learning. Therefore, it appeared appropriate to consider the parent as he functions in his role as educator, and to study how the Montessori method could be implemented in the home.

This pamphlet demonstrates how Maria Montessori's ideas can be put into practice by presenting actual instances of what has been attempted and found to be successful. Through this material, readers have an opportunity to assess for themselves the value of this approach.

Maria Montessori stressed observation of the child as basic to an understanding of him and as the essential ingredient for developing appropriate methods to aid him. Such stress on observation is emphasized throughout this booklet; the more formal outlines are only a guide. The parent must always be alert to new patterns of behavior and to what clues they give about the child's level of development. With some reading and a desire to see one's child as he really is, this part of the approach is not only achieved with little difficulty, but it becomes a most gratifying endeavor. Many have found it to be just plain fun.

The basic orientation and philosophy of the parent is of great importance. How does he look upon others? Does he see each person as having worth and dignity in his own right? If he holds this view at the verbal level, to what extent is it operational at the behavioral level? Does the parent tend to treat the child as a person of worth or does he subtly devalue him? Does he respect the child's capacity and his right of self-direction? The answers to such questions are important as the basic determinants of the nature of a parent's method of approach.

The history of philosophy teaches us that mind and body cannot be viewed separately; we now see that this is true for little people—right from birth. When our children ask for food, we feed them; when they need love and affection, we are there to nurture them; and now, when they ask to learn before the age of six years, we know we cannot starve them intellectually. The cry of educators, philosophers, and psychologists is, "meet your child's needs." That is precisely the goal this pamphlet is striving for. Our hope is that it will spur others to look positively on the work that can and should be done in the home to help turn the young child into the productive adult.

PART I.

A PRELIMINARY STUDY

We approach the task of child-rearing depending on instinct to carry us through and discover that we possess only an abysmal ignorance. The current child-care texts prove to be handy ready references but they give no long view, no perspective, no principles that can be applied to a circumstance that hasn't been detailed. The mother is only more perplexed if her particular problem is not discussed or if the specific answer doesn't work in her case.

Since our mechanical conveniences are giving us freedom from drudgery, let us use the time and energy to focus on the child and ourselves, not anxiously, but in a spirit of wonder. Dr. Maria Montessori does offer a concept of the child, a concept of motherhood, and general principles of guidance.

THE WORK OF THE CHILD

What is the small child? A pure soul, a growing body, and an absorbent mind? He is all these and more. He is a human being needful of respect as well as love, needful of work more than play, and needful of freedom as much as direction.

These principles of respect for the individuality of the child, of permitting him to work at his full capacity, and of granting him freedom from parental interruptions, these are Maria Montessori's ideas which can be written in great letters as guidelines for parents of the pre-school child.

The parents' work begins at birth. It starts with watching the child, with trying to understand and meet his needs as they develop—the need for affection, independence, and order—and never blocking his groping for these means of self-growth.

The child's need for love is instinctively satisfied by most parents, but his later need for independence (beginning a little before two) may bring forth a parental attitude of "mother knows best and can do it better."

The child is directed by God. The individuality of both parents *and* child must be preserved during these early years. In *Education for a New World*, Maria Montessori says that we must help a child to do his *own* acting, willing, and thinking.

Montessori spoke again and again of the "work of the child" which quite simply *is to make himself into an adult*. He does it himself; the parents cannot do it for him. He does most of it before he is six and more than half before he is three. Adults can help or hinder as with any growing thing, but are warned that "every unnecessary help is a hindrance."

The Need for Independence

Perhaps the most important point for a parent to remember is never to help the child when he can help himself. Self-help leads to self-mastery.

A child works slowly, deliberately, joyfully. He must have time enough to complete his project. So the adult has to learn patience and respect for this lack of hurry. The child repeats because of an inner need for growth. Work refreshes him instead of tiring him because he is creating himself. While the aim of the adult's work is external-accomplishment, the aim of the child's work is internal-growth, the perfection of self.

The work the child tries to do has to hold out a promise of success. He should achieve at his own level, at his own rhythm, and according to his own needs.

Every parent can give his child freedom to act independently when he wants to dress or undress himself, to feed himself, to set the table, etc. Liberty of this sort is not permissiveness.

The Sensitive Periods

The Montessori parent should also be aware of the sensitive periods of development, those periods when a child's nature is most ready to receive a particular kind of knowledge. Generally, Montessori expects children to be able to do more at an earlier age than is commonly expected. In the broad sense, she says that the years from birth to six, particularly those from three to six, are the years for the construction of memory, reason, and will. This is the time for the construction of the ability to make a free choice, for the construction of the individual. The child during these years is not yet truly a social being. He is still engaged in making himself.

The sensitive periods have a sequence almost as rigid as the development within the womb. The following might be said to be a parent's timetable of such periods:

- 0–3 The absorbent mind. The child teaches himself.
- ½–3 Language (second language, too)
- 1½   Complicated activities (carrying heavy objects, etc.); Growth of attention and coordination
- 1½–4 Love of very small objects (involves sense of wonder and praise)
- 2–4 Order in time and space
- 2–4 Truth and reality (no fairy tales yet)
- 2½–6 Refinement of the senses (pitch, color, etc.)
- 3–6 The child is more susceptible to adult influences.
- 3½–4½ Writing (the mind and the muscles are ready). He cares for drawing or handling geometric shapes.
- 4–4½ Tactile sense
- 4½–5½ Reading

Education of the Child

Each man makes a fresh start. Man's distinction is the long infancy which makes possible the fresh start. All other living things follow the pattern of their predecessors or else a new fixed pattern set by mutation, but any human cultural pattern is possible for the baby at birth. A newborn baby from one of the primitive Stone Age tribes could be brought up in an industrial nation and make the transition with perfect success.

There are three characteristics of what Maria Montessori calls good in the education of the child—Freedom; Concentration; and Sense of reality. How to give a person true freedom; how to teach him to concentrate; how to accustom him to the correction of the real world; how to develop the true use of free will and understanding—these were her preoccupations.

Montessori asserts that a child's predisposition is to—exactness; detail; and complexity. For example, when the child begins to talk the parent should know that in teaching both pronunciation and vocabulary the hunger for exactness can be fed; when this has been done the child's ability to be precise has been strengthened for that time whenever the child-become-adult will need such ability. And when the child is learning to walk, or to tumble, or to work with his hands, parents should keep in mind the little games of walking along a line, of fitting toys together, of carrying out a sequence of activity to completion. All of these have the long-range goal of feeding intellectual hunger for exactness, detail, and complexity.

The education of the senses is a very important part of teaching the child. The parent can make a game of the lesson. He can use bells, for instance, for training the ear, or different fabrics for teaching the ability to distinguish by touch, even hot bread or French perfume to stimulate interest in identifying through the sense of smell. There is a pattern of teaching to be followed in such lessons. First, the child should be attracted to the "props" which, in turn, must be graded in stimuli. The names should be used with all the objects, and if possible, each particular sense should be isolated during such lesson periods.

A parent teaching a child to recognize an object by touch rather than by sight, for example, could ask him to reach into a drawstring bag for odd objects and to designate each by name from its shape or texture before withdrawing his hand from the bag.

Special teaching materials, somewhat similar to the Montessori classroom equipment, can often be made at home or occasionally purchased. Many manufacturers of children's educational toys, however, have not yet learned Montessori's rule of isolation of stimulus. For instance, they will confuse a study in size with a change in color, too.

In the years from one to three, when a child's whole being is most ready to learn a language, even a second language can be introduced, particularly if one or both parents have fluency in several languages. Montessori reminds us that in learning to speak a child also lays the foundations for his particular religion and national and social sentiment.

The Need for Order

Maria Montessori emphasized repeatedly in all of her writings a child's need for order. The need for order is perhaps a constant throughout life, but between the ages of two to four the first foundations helping to meet this need should be laid. Some time during this two-year span every parent meets the child's insistent, inflexible demand for order. This is one of the sensitive periods mentioned by Montessori easiest to recognize and utilize.

To instill the concept of order in the mind of the child calls for definite rules: (a) An object used by a child must be returned to its original place in its original order after the child has finished with it; (b) Anything begun must be finished; and (c) Order includes good manners, based on respect for others.

The Prepared Environment

Up until the age of six a prepared environment provides both a practical arrangement for orderly living for the child and an atmosphere of peace in which he can learn.

The home environment can be prepared so that through freedom to perform social exercises in real situations, such as setting a table, serving himself a simple meal, dressing himself, caring for a pet, tending a garden, the child learns not only order and an orderly routine of life, but carefulness, consideration, observation, and patience. He is learning how to perform adult love for others and tending away from selfishness towards selflessness.

The parent should keep in mind that children like to work, even at the tender age of two, if it is properly presented. For the very young the chief thing to remember is that they are not concerned about getting done. The child is really happy polishing and polishing and polishing. Economy of effort belongs to the adult way of looking at things. If the parents can let the child work with joy, skill will come and be available later. Montessori says that by his own interest in any activity the adult gives it dignity and solemnity. The first preparation of the environment really takes place in the mind of the parent. *His* work is twofold: he should give the child the proper working conditions, and he should be an adult.

On the tangible side of preparing the environment, parents can arrange the bedroom or playroom with child-sized furniture, low pegs in the closet for him to hang up his own clothes, tools for imitating the action of the adults around him, and shelves for toys and other possessions (there is no order possible in a toy box). One parent who provided an orderly arrangement reported that during a room repainting session, when all furniture, shelves, and toys were stacked together in the hall, their little girl refused to touch anything.

As the child attempts to duplicate the work of his parents, his confidence in himself should not be shaken by having the work done over in his presence.

When thinking about the environment in which a child thrives, of more importance than toy shelves, closet pegs, or small chairs is an atmosphere of calmness and quiet. The child should be sheltered from the hustling world —the bustling mother.

He must also have freedom from interruptions, the freedom to concentrate and work in his own way when he wishes. The Montessori classroom teacher does not interrupt the child even to praise him.

Dangerous activities are forbidden to the child and explained as far as possible. In the adult world there are rules to follow, and so, too, in the child's world. A world revolving entirely around the child is not reality; it is not preparation for adulthood, which is the child's goal as well as the parents'.

Summary

From the pages of Maria Montessori's writings we can make a list of her findings on the characteristics of the pre-school child. He prefers work to play, order to disorder, silence to noise, self-mastery to dependence on others, mutual aid to competition. He is a joyous, sometimes ecstatic, sometime serious, little creature. He is capable of profound spontaneous concentration, of sublimating possessiveness, of acting from real choice rather than idle curiosity, and of obedience. And he has a strong attachment to reality while still being able to hear underground rivers and see minute blue bugs while his parent hears a bus and sees only a broken sidewalk.

THE WORK OF THE PARENT

One of the fundamental keys to the development of the child's intellect and will, and to building a foundation for later character growth is the attitude and understanding of the parent. A disciplined yet "active" environment which is responsive to the needs of the child is the other essential factor.

The parent as teacher has three areas to examine and re-examine—himself; the child; and the surrounding environment.

Attitude and Understanding of the Parent

The parent must first look to himself, to examine his attitude towards the child. Attitudes are reflected in the way a parent speaks to a child and the manner in which he respects every member of the family as an individual.

Children absorb the love which surrounds them and it is through the actions and attitudes of their parents, especially, that they incorporate certain intellectual, spiritual, and moral values. The seven cardinal virtues must be practiced in the home first, before they will be imitated by the child. Parents are the models for imitation. They must be capable of silence, patience, and respect for others if they want their children to acquire these qualities. The parent must be aware of how he reacts, of how he approaches his job, and then be willing to reorganize himself and remove those attitudes which stunt the child's growth of imagination and which frustrate the inner need to develop.

Just as the surrounding materials do not hurry the child or interrupt him, but invite him to learn so also should the parent in his daily life be inviting and a joy to the child in his work and inner development.

Observation of the Child

Dr. Montessori's ideas were revolutionary. She advocated that the child be left alone to think in peace and that he be given the opportunity to be himself. The parent must guard this ability to think. Once the child finds himself he will be capable of caring about others; because he as an individual has been respected, he will respect others; he will learn how to love because he, himself, has been surrounded by adult love.

The child reveals himself to us and the parent should ask himself, "What is the child teaching me?" From the beginning the parent should observe not only the physical development of the infant, but the expressions on his face which indicate mental growth. The child's expressions and reactions develop into meaningful patterns as time goes on. Only by knowing the child as much as possible is the parent able to become familiar with his modes of behavior. If the adult is busy trying to impose his will on the child, not only will the child profit little, but the parent will know very little about his own child.

It is imperative for the parent to observe each child and ask himself questions: "What is the child teaching me?" "Why did the child either lose interest or else suddenly take the initiative?" "What were the surrounding circumstances that encouraged this behavior?" For example: the child who drops a toy repeatedly and waits for his mother to return it may be doing an exercise in depth perception.

Montessori Characteristics

Dr. Montessori called attention to certain characteristics in the 2-6 year old which are of special value. Three of these follow: When a child between the ages of 2-6 sits quietly on occasion and is seemingly peaceful, he is manifesting one of these characteristics. He is not bored, for there is complete serenity as he stops his activity and perhaps rests on the floor or couch with his toys about him. A possible explanation is that the body is resting so that the mind may absorb all that the child is learning so rapidly. It may even be Nature's way of providing mental reflection, although the child is not conscious of such a mental process taking place. During such quiet times the parent should not interfere; rather, notice what the surrounding circumstances were so as to encourage more quiet times. Such contemplative periods are invaluable for later life, for it may be said that they prepare the child to enter into a private world of meditation and mental calm with God.

Another trait especially valued by Montessori is shown when the child initiates some activity of his own. This initiative is evident when the child is completely absorbed in his activity. There is a spontaneity in his choice of work, a display of earnest concentration, and a peace of spirit as the child completes his cycle of activity without being interrupted.

A third characteristic valued by Montessori is the child who is spontaneously helpful or polite without the parent urging him or reminding him. Again, the parent should look to the circumstances that prompted such activity. Oftentimes it is an imitation of home environment. Nevertheless, the adult can learn a great deal from children for they seem to possess a fine power of discrimination as to when to help, encourage, or comfort one another. They seem to distinguish between the child able to manage and the one in real need of help.

The Home Environment

The physical environment is the third area for parents to consider. It should be set up so as to invite and permit the child to develop his own inner resources: "The environment is to reveal, not mold, the child."

In the Montessori class the child is taught how to master his movements: how to walk quietly, how to lift a small table and set it down, how to move a chair, how to execute all the simple gestures of living; first with exaggerated care and then in an unconsciously careful way, as he masters each pattern of movement.

The Parent as a Teacher

In teaching a new skill or introducing new material to work with, the parent should sit down at the child's side and make sure he has his undivided attention. Explanations should be short, simply stated, and to the point. If words are necessary use only the minimum and none at all if demonstration alone will get the lesson across. Words often distract and interfere with concentration.

It is important to do the whole exercise in front of the child. Never stop in the middle of an exercise and assume that the child will know how to do the whole lesson.

The child's attention is to be focused on the object, not on the parent; her personality should disappear. The child's eyes should be on the object itself and on the parent's hands which are manipulating it. If the child becomes distracted, wait until you have his attention again before going on with the exercise. If the child is not interested, *do not* insist on repeating the lesson or making the child understand that he has made a mistake or not understood. Just put away the object for another time.

In teaching a skill, isolate the difficulties. This is what is meant by step learning. Present one difficulty at a time. For example, when teaching a child how to tie a shoe, work on just the lacing one day, on making the knot the next day, and on tying the bow the following day.

Interference or Interruption

When should we as parents interfere? We should interrupt when the child reveals to us that he is not capable of handling a situation or controlling himself. Any activity that is destructive or harmful to others should not be allowed. A good rule is to isolate the child from the thing that he is incapable of leaving alone. Parents should interfere and sometimes quite strongly when the occasion calls for it.

It is the duty of the parent to look at the child that he is bringing up; he must free himself to be with the child when the child is in need of the adult. Often it calls for reorganization of one's schedule. Is it not the child to whom the parent is dedicating his very life, work, effort, and thought?

A Lesson in Detail: The Three Steps of Seguin

The ideal is to have a quiet work area for it helps to promote spontaneous activity and isolates the working child from the rest of the activity of the house. Dr. Montessori speaks of each child working on a small rug. Such an area helps to develop a sense of order within the child along with giving him the privacy he needs.

Parents cannot and should not aim for the detail of the classroom in the home, for the individuality of the home is important and something to be preserved.

A child's desire for activity shows an inner need that must be met and satisfied. The parent at first needs to direct and guide the child's activities, but once he becomes absorbed in a task he should be left alone, because in this state of absorption he is at the same time both creating and discovering the powers of his own intellect.

Here is an example of the *three steps of Seguin,* used in learning numbers 1-10:

a) Parent pointing to rods:

This is one	This is two	This is three
/	//	///

b) Parent says to the child:

    Point to two   Point to one   Point to three

c) Having rearranged the order of the rods, the parent asks:

    What is this?   What is that?

This sequence for learning is used for teaching many words and ideas. In the first step the parent says the word and points to one of several objects. In the second step the parent says the word but the child points. In the last step the child does both pointing and speaking.

1) This is a maple leaf (or a triangle, or Asia, etc.).
2) Which is the maple leaf (or triangle or Asia, etc.)?
3) What is this? What is that?

Silence

The concepts of silence, politeness, and composure must first be understood before they can be practiced by the child. Dr. Montessori emphasizes that silence is a most profound activity. She taught silence through various exercises of silence. Once she let the children experience silence by observing a four month old infant. She called the infant the little teacher and brought out that no one could keep so still as the infant nor breathe so silently. She then invited the children to come close up on tiptoe. When leaving the room, Dr. Montessori reminded the children that the infant went with her in silence and that she herself made noise even though she was walking "quietly." The next lesson was for the children to "make" silence. She reminded them that a foot that moves makes noise. She held their attention and then called them by name in a gentle voice and as each child was called he stood up silently, trying not to move his chair, and walked toward her on tiptoe. The lesson called for self-control, attention, and coordination of muscles, but the children were learning the real and complete meaning of silence.

"HUMAN DIGNITY IS BORN OF THE SENTIMENT OF ONE'S INDEPENDENCE"

Everyone, of course, is in favor of freedom. But our problem is to consider precisely what Montessori meant by independence and how she said it was to be attained. To her it had two aspects. There was the technique of laying the foundation. There was the final construction of the adult.

The Free Adult

Let us consider the second aspect first. The independent adult as she saw him and tried to produce him in her schools had many skills. He had superior academic training and was accustomed to intellectual pursuits. He had fluent use of his own language, written and spoken, and also of a foreign tongue. He understood mathematics. He knew history and religion and his place in the world. He had musical training. He had the freedom that comes from habitual good manners and grace in getting along with others. *He was accustomed to choosing for himself.*

Free will and understanding, then, were in good working order. How had this been done? We would love to be able to make long observations of a method that hopes for such results. But from reading we can summarize a few principles.

Free Will for the Children

The ability to make a free choice is said to depend on wide experience as well as on permission to choose. Therefore small children should have a wide variety of activities offered within their prepared environment, and they must be allowed to choose freely among these possibilities. This can be put into practice at home.

When they were given free choice of an occupation in an environment where it was possible to learn the use of letters and numbers, it became clear that the three and four year olds had a great interest and indeed that this was the easiest time for them to begin to learn the three R's. Surprisingly, writing precedes reading. To do this at home would require correct materials, correct technique, and courage to differ from the present community pattern.

After reading has been acquired, many freedoms follow.

> And this bequest of wings
> Was but a book—

Muscular Coordination

Training in precise motions for all the activities of daily life is pleasing to the small children. Precision pleases them. Through practice, muscular coordination is acquired and this mastery of their own muscles makes them happy. It is supposed to be the reason why they are in no hurry to finish a task. The mother has a superior opportunity to teach this coordination by encouraging precise ways in speaking, in dressing, and in caring for the immediate environment.

The command to be precise in daily activities sometimes seems troubling. The experience of most mothers seems to be that meticulous housekeeping is not possible all day long and every day. We feel that two considerations are in order here. Precision in at least some activities may be enough to lay the foundation. Second, one of Montessori's most startling discoveries was that the three year olds have a passion for order and were her most valuable allies in keeping things precisely in place.

Montessori might have approved some of the Japanese customs of housekeeping, such as leaving shoes outside, or keeping a room bare of everything except the immediate activity.

Imitation and the Growing Will

After the initial development of coordination, the child may try imitating. This is really a manifestation of the growing will, which is trying to obtain command of the muscles. At this time it is an exercise which helps the will grow stronger. Later there will come self-planned activities and reasoned action.

Obedience and the Growing Will

After the child is able to command *himself,* because he possesses the physical ability to accompany his will, he is able to practice obedience, which is accepting the will of another. Obedience cannot come sooner. This obedience is necessary to the extensive learning which is a part of adult independence.

Concentration

The activity which may be considered to sum up all these others of coordination, imitation, willing, reasoned action, and obedience is concentration. *"The first essential for the child's development is concentration."* (The italics are ours.)

Our task is to provide an environment adapted to the child's needs—one he can cope with. He needs tangible things on which to focus his attention. Montessori said that a limited space helped concentration. She felt that instruction should come from materials when possible, rather than from a person. As an example of this, we felt that the coloring books that are colored on one page were silent instruction and correction. In addition to adequate materials for concentration, the child needs freedom from interruption. The mother must find means of guarding the concentration of her child from her own intrusion or too many visitors.

Growth in independence, then, comes from activity and experience, and we are to provide opportunities to exercise the will, for its growth depends on its being used.

Freedom Defined

In the encyclical of Leo XIII called *Libertas Praestantissimum* it was stated:
1. Only those who have the gift of reason can have true freedom.
2. Liberty is the faculty of choosing means fitted for the end purpose.
3. Every act of true choice is preceded by an act of judgment.
4. Because of the imperfection of man's nature a law is necessary to point out the way in conformity with reason.
5. One who acts through a power outside himself is a slave.

EDUCATION OF THE SENSES AND MOVEMENT
THE BASIS OF THE MONTESSORI METHOD

"Nothing is in the intellect which is not first in the senses." Dr. Montessori, as so many psychologists and psychiatrists are doing today, developed her principles around the teachings of Saint Thomas Aquinas. The basis of the Montessori Method is contact and exploration of the environment through the senses and movement.

There are two levels of learning, unconscious and conscious, with a chronological division. Zero to three years is the time of unconscious learning, with conscious learning beginning around three.

Montessori has given the meaningful name Absorbent Mind to the period of unconscious learning. By explanation an analogy is drawn between the mind and a camera which takes a picture of a large crowd or of an entire landscape as readily as it does of a single object.

Because the child has had no sensory experience, he comes into the world without a single idea in his mind. He will, by the spontaneous activity of his intellect, gain for himself knowledge of a spoken language, concepts of time, space, cause and effect from the environment in which he is placed.

This tremendous knowledge comes to the child without any seeming effort on his part. We cannot fathom the mysterious ability of his inner teacher that works so ceaselessly, so unerringly, on a time schedule so perfect that pediatricians can put a chart on the office wall timetabling the predicted developmental progress of the average child. It behooves the parent to regard this awesome mechanism within the child with a respect that gives one a clear sense of each child's individuality, of his yet unmeasured potential. It is a time when the parent will provide a rich background in every area from play to moral values to nourish this eager teacher working within the child.

Going into the fourth year the child shows, with the gradual emergence of consciousness, a need, and with the gradual emergence of the will an ability, to bring order and clarity to the great wealth of knowledge absorbed and accumulated in the first years of life. This is the time when Montessori introduces the child to a programme for educating the senses and movement. Her method outlines the way that this can best be done with scientific apparatus and exercises.

The training of the senses while fulfilling the need of the child at the time, is broadening the field of perception to establish a rich and solid base for the functioning of the mind. The evidence of the child's desire to categorize and classify corresponds to the time when fundamental habits of intelligence are formed. The exact way of training the senses, then, is typical of a basic Montessori principle of offering the best material in the best way at the best time.

Montessori states that the ability to "express an idea in action" is the main function of the mind. This ability to act is the beginning of the will, or of the character development which is prerequisite to learning. Again in the education of movement there is a specific time to initiate the materials and exercises for the analysis of movement. As with the senses the groundwork is laid in the first years of life.

By observing the child a parent can realize the needs of the child at each particular stage. Recognizing these stages and providing the child with the means of satisfying his fundamental interest in a certain exercise of movement makes these times, that might otherwise be difficult, fun for all.

The child's need for big muscle experience and development is apparent when he spends a large part of his day attempting to climb on furniture, bounce on his bed, carry objects so large as to be staggering. It is the time to provide for these needs in a safe, convenient way so as to prevent feelings of frustration or guilt on the part of the child.

There is the period when the child is most interested in learning to move about, to become master of his actions. Later he will be less interested in muscular coordination, careless about precision in movement. This is the time when Montessori begins education of movement, or the analysis of successive movements distinct from one another. The beginnings of this may be seen in practical life exercises, such as pouring from a pitcher, buttoning, turning a key in the lock.

In the Montessori classroom there is always to be found a line on the floor in the form of an ellipse. The exercises on the line are succeedingly more difficult. After walking the line carefully placing one foot before the other, heel to toe, the child will walk carrying a flag, then a glass of water, then a bell. If the attention of the child wanders the flag will be lowered, the water may spill, or the bell ring, helping the child concentrate on his precise movement.

FROM SIX TO TWELVE

Introduction

Maria Montessori calls the childhood age from six to twelve a period of great stability, a time of growth without transformation. Because there is comparative calm and serenity, children of this age group are capable of making great strides in the work of the mind and in the acquisition of culture.

General Characteristics—6 to 12

The general characteristics of the six to twelve age group may be divided into physical, intellectual, and social. Physically, it is a time for rugged outdoor play. Socially, we see that the personality grows more complex, the herd instinct comes out and there is a constantly growing interest in other people and their ideas.

In speaking of intellectual growth, it can almost be said that there is a timetable.

Six is a fertile field for all factors of culture—the seeds sown will germinate later.
Seven is able to learn the nomenclature of many fields of science.
Nine is ready to probe mathematics—algebra, geometry, and the extraction of square roots.
Ten. By the time a child in a Montessori school reaches the age of ten he is expected to speak two languages fluently, and to be able to read and write Latin.

In general, between six and twelve, a child's ability to reason is constantly growing. However, *groups of related facts* should be presented to the child's mind, not isolated facts. A child at the bottom of this age group cannot be expected to understand or to see relationships fully, but the ability to see different sides of a question grows as the child reaches 10 or 11.

A Time of Calm?

Montessori stressed this age period as being one of great stability—a time of calm and serenity for the child. However, in contradiction to Montessori, Gesell states that the ages of seven and nine are years of anxieties, worries, and insecurities.

The years of anxieties and insecurities of which Gesell speaks might be the product of too little preparation in the early years for the independence that is suddenly thrust upon our children when they enter the first grade of school. So often a young child is alternately coddled and made to feel a nuisance. The feeling of being a truly contributing member of the family should carry over to the school and life in general. This would enable him to adjust to all the new things he will find in the early school years. The feeling of confidence and independence achieved through the knowledge of many small obstacles overcome in earlier years can be the key to tranquility in the years six to twelve.

Starvation of the mind during early "sensitive periods" could also be a reason for the stresses of these later years. Montessori says that the child of six loves to learn all of the new words that there are for him to experiment with. The reading experience of the child in the first grade text is usually severely limited. For this particular problem it would be the responsibility of the parent to provide an enrichment of the child's experience.

Moral Judgments become Possible

Maria Montessori, in her book *To Educate the Human Potential*, makes four major points about the child aged six to twelve. The first is that moral judgments are possible; the second, that the prepared environment becomes restrictive; the third, that the child seeks groups; and the fourth, that teachers and parents must make the right use of the child's imagination.

In the area of moral judgments, we find that a teacher's or parent's opinions and ideas are very important to the child, but there is a steady growth of his own ideas of right and wrong. There also develops a clear understanding of individual property rights. Unlike the very young child, a child during this period begins to foresee what consequences his actions may bring and has an increasing ability to plan ahead. Abstract ideas of justice and honor begin to have meaning for the child and he is able to understand religious principles or, for example, a Scout code.

The Prepared Environment becomes Restrictive

The special environment which in earlier years the child had accepted as his own special and beloved world is now restrictive and the child seeks and needs the outdoors and new experiences. This is the time of caves and tree houses, or of gardening, which can teach the child all the factors of soil, water, weather, and care which enter into the growth of plants. Through the care of animals a child can learn a sense of responsibility and concern. A small brother or sister can teach responsibility and concern for others in a much more pertinent way.

The Child Seeks Groups

The love of being part of a group at this age leads to the formation of all kinds of clubs. Some may have for their sole objective to keep others out.

There is a great love of outdoor play and games, but the child may become an onlooker rather than a participator if motor skills are not developed. Here there is a needed follow-through on the Montessori ideas of physical exercises for the pre-schooler.

During the six to twelve period a child progresses from having a friend or two, to belonging to a group, to group activities, and finally, to team work and spirit. The Boy Scout movement is closest to Montessori's ideal of education at this age through using the child's natural instinct for groups. In the Scout movement the child is encouraged to act efficiently and independently. There are tests to be passed and disciplines to be mastered.

The Right Use of the Imagination

Montessori encouraged fairy tales at this older age. For younger children she feared a confusion of the sense of reality, but at this age she felt that the children were ready for the poetic and moral truth of the tales. For example, *Cinderella* is the truest story that we know! The pumpkin, rats, and mice are our human acts, useless to fulfill our hope of love and heaven until transformed by the grace of God.

But the mind and imagination are more stimulated and knowledge is made more coherent by a study of the universe, of the whole realm of physical and natural science. This was a startling thought in 1910 when Montessori proposed it. With Col. Glenn's flight it is clear that a new age has begun and enthusiasm is ready.

In teaching a child of the creation of the earth keep in mind that facts, such as the geological formation or the early amphibians or the glacial age, are less interesting to the child than how they were discovered. A child is tremendously interested in the accounts of how anthropologists and archaeologists made their great discoveries. He is also greatly impressed by sheer size; one should mention figures for the depth of the ocean, the numbers of stars, the vastness of space. This will help to give a proper sense of wonder.

A FINAL WORD TO PART I

This pamphlet is a record of discussions on *Montessori in the Home* that covered half a year. Members of the group had many years of experience in caring for children. About a third of the group did the actual writing.

There were two aims in presenting this pamphlet. The first was to arouse the curiosity of parents so that they would read Montessori's own books. The second was to provoke consideration of mothers' and fathers' ideal role in light of Montessori's discoveries concerning the growth of the human mind.

Until the formal Montessori materials and techniques are more readily available, we place all our emphasis on this statement:

> Seize every opportunity that presents itself to develop the child's independence, concentration, and sense of reality.

The authors of Part I are: Cecelia Dougherty, Margaret Jackson, Sarah Jackson, Evelyn McQuie, Martha O'Keefe, Marilyn Schwartz, and Marian Williams.

PART II.

PRACTICAL APPLICATION

WRITING AND READING

Many skills make up the ability to write and to read. A child must learn to talk, to spell, to hold a pencil, to form letters, to recognize letters at sight. These skills do not develop overnight. After a good beginning, gradual improvement comes over a period of years. If reading and writing are mastered at about the age of six, that is about right on Montessori's timetable, since English is not phonetically spelled. Mastery at six is quite a different matter from beginning at six.

The skills to be considered in this chapter fall into four main categories: pronunciation or "sound spelling," penmanship, composing, and reading. Let us consider them in that order, realizing that they are introduced to the child simultaneously.

Pronunciation

The way to begin is to help the child learn to speak. We know little about what makes a child speak at one time instead of another. But some practical advice can be given. The child should hear careful speech. The pronunciation should be clear, the grammar correct, the tone pleasant.

There is a time when children crave the spoken word and will sit contentedly listening to anything. The adult may read out loud from his own book or newspaper or magazine, or he may choose great poetry.

In time, of course, one must read children's stories. These should be chosen carefully. The child who is ready for such stories may ask for constant repetition. Repeat for him, if possible. He is very likely memorizing the entire content.

We discovered an interesting exercise in pronunciation. Several children, at about the age of two or two and a half, were interested in repeating words after an adult.

"Will you read to me?" "Yes, would you like to say it after me?" The adult would read three or four words (or more, after several months), and the child would repeat them. This had the surprising effect of causing the child to pronounce sounds that he might otherwise have avoided. In this situation, as at almost any time when a word is mispronounced, the parent says, "Look at me," and then pronounces the word, sound by sound.

If the child is interested, he will work at learning to pronounce for a long time.

The technique of teaching pronunciation by getting down to the child's eye-level and pronouncing slowly sound-by-sound leads directly to a Montessori game called "sound-spelling." The game can begin by having the child put letters from the movable alphabet around the room: s for sofa, r for rug, t for table, w for window, b for bookshelf, etc. Letters could be written on small slips of paper for the same game; this method makes it easier to assert that ch is for chair.

A later game is to look at pictures and sound-spell the words (be sure to pronounce only the letter, not an extra "uh" sound), or to think of words such as the names of whatever we see in books or through windows. These words are sometimes sound-spelled and sometimes "spelled" with the movable alphabet. This is still phonetic spelling, and it should not be corrected if it is phonetically correct—unless the child should ask, as he may if he has become aware of the trickiness of English spelling. If he asks, answer truthfully.

Letters in the movable alphabet are from 1½ to 2½ inches high—about ½ the size of the sandpaper letters. They may be cut out or written on small cards. Use of this alphabet makes it possible to write words or sentences before penmanship is mastered.

The astonishing rule is that the child can learn to "write" with the movable alphabet months before he can read. Therefore, *do not* ask him to read whatever he has just written. If you do, he may cry or turn away from his interest in writing.

When the child can write letters, he may continue to make up lists of words. No longer bound by the bulky movable alphabet, he may sit near his busy parents and write lists of rhyming words such as ice, rice, nice or ink, pink, link, sink, etc.

The transition from phonetic spelling to correct spelling will be discussed later in this chapter.

Penmanship

The first preparation that Montessori offered for penmanship was the use of small knobs on the earliest didactic apparatus. The precise use of the small finger muscles to hold tiny things, such as knobs and pencils, was thus developed.

The second preparation was the geometric cabinet. The use of this cabinet is discussed in detail in the chapter on the didactic materials. It is a very important part of the Montessori method.

An interesting testimony to the value of work with the geometric figures is found in a study made in Winter Haven, Florida, and reported in *The Nation's Schools* in February 1962. According to this report:

"Readiness for formal learning is more than a product of sheer growth. The child first must be taught literally to learn to get 'ready' for the more formal experience in a course of study. As an example, behind the capacity to deal with communicative symbolic form must be a developed capacity to understand and manipulate simple forms, such as circles, squares, triangles, and so forth.

Several investigators have shown that guided experience in drawing elementary forms, such as circles, squares, and triangles, given to beginning school children significantly advances their readiness for more complex form recognition tasks, such as reading. These were not merely the older activities of practicing recognition of form likes and differences, but involved *actual directed practice* in drawing as well as identifying form."

In working with the geometric cabinet, the child first learns the names of the forms. He learns to feel the insets with his fingers and to replace them in the frames blindfolded. He learns that a fine line may represent a whole solid inset. And he traces around the insets. The tracing may be done with colored pencils, and it may be filled in with another color. The first exercise in filling in a tracing is to make a zigzag line from bottom to top and from left to right:

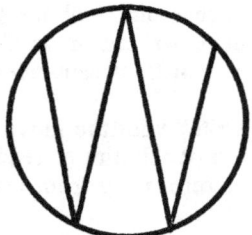  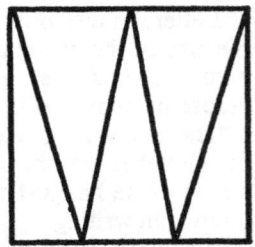

The child will need plenty of practice before he can stop at the border. The mother might say: "May I show you something?" If he agrees, she should do the whole tracing carefully. "Would you like to try it?" He does it, but not very well. Then she says, "May I have a turn," and she does it very attentively and correctly. "Do you want to do it again?"

The child will probably need many days to master the straight lines. So long as he is trying, he should be let alone. There is a Montessori rule that says that misuse of materials should not be allowed. This rule can be seriously abused. As long as the child thinks he is trying to do the exercise, he should be let alone. Brief demonstrations by the parent from day to day when he has both time and the child's attention should be enough.

The tracings may be completely filled with parallel lines when a little skill has been developed. A figure three or four inches in diameter is too much to tackle at once, so it should be divided into less overwhelming bits:

FIRST STEP   **SECOND STEP**

This can be very attractive in different colors and is pleasing to the child as he struggles for precision and mastery of his muscles. Once the child has mastered these exercises the challenge of something more complicated, such as the superimposition of the shapes into interesting designs, can be presented.

He should also be allowed plenty of free time for use of pencils, crayons, tracing paper, stencils, and whatever seems fun. Mothers will want to devise some way to keep the writing on the paper, not on the walls. The obvious solution is supervision, but supervision is not easy if the mother is busy with an infant or with demanding tasks. Each mother must find her own solution, but we would regret a solution which permanently banned an opportunity to scribble or color.

A next step is the use of the sandpaper letters, which teach the eye, the ear, the mouth, and the hand. The sandpaper letter is to be traced with two fingers in the order in which it is written. As the child traces the letter, he also sounds it. This tracing helps to make a clear distinction between such letters as *b* and *p*. Teach the letters a few at a time, using the three steps of Seguin. Let the child set his own pace as to how many to learn each day. Be sure to pronounce only the letter, not an extra "uh" sound. The transition to reading is easier if the child thinks, for example, that *p-a-t* makes three sounds but not three *syllables*.

The letters may be capitals. However, we prefer lower case script sandpaper letters, in the hope of producing legible penmanship. There is not yet conclusive evidence that one choice is better than the other for the beginning. The child must, of course, learn all four alphabets some day—script and print, capitals and lower case.

After the child has learned the letters, he may "write" them in various ways. Letters in the air are always "perfect." Letters may be written in fingerpaint. They may be written on paper with a pencil.

When the letters can be written, they may be used to replace the movable alphabet in the games of making words or lists of words.

Composing

A third skill may be called composing. The first exercises are for the parents to read aloud a great deal and to talk enough. Next, they should be an attentive, responsive audience who encourage accurate reporting as well as accurate pronunciation and correct grammar. Made up stories are all right if the child distinguishes clearly between fact and fancy. Montessori did not believe that the sense of reality should be dimmed or confused.

The child who has learned to make clear sentences can write compositions either with the movable alphabet or by hand when his penmanship is ready.

Word Recognition

First, the child should be read to.

Second, he should see that the people around him value reading themselves. Parents should avoid getting so enmeshed in chores that their children never see them reading.

Sometimes in using the sandpaper letters or movable alphabet, the child will merely look at them and name them, rather than moving his hand over them. This sight recognition is "reading." This kind of reading will doubtless lead to questions about traffic signs, grocery labels, and other large letters in the environment.

Montessori used to write "command slips," on which the writing would tell the child to do something. Following these written commands can give the child a great deal of satisfaction and fun.

The mysteries of English spelling must be met. A good system is to prepare a series of small booklets. Fold a sheet of typing paper several times and stitch or staple it in the middle, adding a construction paper cover. On the cover of each booklet, write a phonogram, such as *ai*. On each page, write a word containing *ai*, with the *ai* in one color and the remainder in another. Possible words would be: main, sail, rain, bait, chair, maid, nail, pail, train, wait.

Other booklets can be made for *au, ou, ee, ea* (as in beat, heat), *ea* (as in dead, meadow), *th* (as in this, that), *th* (as in think, thin), *ch, sh, oo* (as in book, foot), *oo* (as in room, boom), *oa, ow, oi, ar, er*.

These booklets will not exhaust the vagaries of English spelling. They will help the beginner, however.

Another help is a list of "puzzle" words or "mystery" words. In a Montessori class, they might be written on slips of paper and drawn from a box for a guessing game. Such words as pigeon, recipe, alphabet, women, lamb, knee, light, cough, and many others can be used.

Children may ask to be read to long after they are well able to read whole books alone. They may ask for this because they are curious about the pronunciation of words. We remember a child who, left to himself, pronounced DEtermined and vociFERously.

If interest and curiosity have been kept alive through all these early years, the child described above should have a good beginning for speaking, writing, and reading well in his own language.

SCIENCE

Perhaps it is in the field of science that the parent is the most surprised at what the small child can accomplish, and also, the most unsure of his own ability to lead. The assimilation of facts which begins in the sensorial age (2-3 years) continues strongly during the period of maximum retention of details, *i.e.,* 3-8 years. The preschool child can be presented with advanced scientific material so long as the form of presentation is adapted to his sensitive periods. Montessori stressed the necessity of activity in the unfolding self. Concentration has its beginnings in work in which the hand and the mind cooperate.

In this discussion we shall try to answer two questions: First, "What can you expect to accomplish in science?" and second, "What do you need to do these things?"

Science should help the child develop a sense of solemn wonder at the order found in nature. He will be looking at the tiny details of law and order in creation and learning to fit them into the cosmic whole.

In any teaching of little children, one must isolate the fact he wishes to teach. For example, one can better teach the parts of a bird with a picture than in nature, and best do it with an inset puzzle so that the small child can feel the configuration as well as see it. Montessori found it better to teach the form of leaves in wooden or cardboard representations than to do so in nature because the color, texture, size, and smell are distracting. Next, names are given to these concepts, *i.e.*, lanceolate, deltoid, pinnate, or bill, crown, upper wing coverts. Now the child is ready to find an acerose leaf or redwing in nature. He will observe more carefully because he understands what he is seeing.

The 2½-3 year old is enthusiastic about minute details, *e.g.*, horned owl versus screech owl, or the edges of leaves, and he is most receptive to proper names. Because of the child's special sensitivity to language, a precise vocabulary is important. Children of 3-6 years have an insatiable thirst for new words. They learn with relish scientific terms which are more difficult for the older child.

It is unfortunate that so many children, and adults, too, neither see nor hear what is occurring around them. The child needs to be encouraged to notice details and then to observe accurately. Walk with your children, even if only around the block, and point out what you pass. Sit in your yard or on a park bench and examine growing things. Look at the people and animals which pass. Listen to the birds or the traffic. Knowledge comes through all our senses, and it is by conscious exercise we refine their powers.

The child should recognize conceptual differences before he gives names to them. The forms of leaves are offered as wooden insets, and when the child can replace the insets correctly, the names are given. A pair of inexpensive beginner collections of minerals can be used as a matching game, so the child may judge the "feel" as well as the appearance before the stones are named. Flashcards are available for birds, flowers, insects, prehistoric animals, etc., which could be used first for matching and then for recognition games. It is important to expose the child to a wide selection of sensory experiences, even though the physical explanations for them are too complex to offer. For example, an awareness that sugar dissolves more easily in hot tea than in the iced beverage and that too much sugar stirred in grandfather's cup will be left at the bottom, help lay the foundation for the study of the physical and chemical properties of matter in solution.

Vocabulary development is the most obvious objective. Nomenclature is offered in the many fields of natural science. These include botany, zoology, mineralogy, geology, chemistry, physics, astronomy, paleontology. To avoid an artificial learning situation, parents might begin with two or three fields in which they feel competent or interested. One needs to feel comfortable in order to be effective.

Now you go forth to collect: leaves, flowers, rocks, pictures of animals seen at the farm or zoo, birds, insects, constellations identified. From the first joyful hodgepodge meaningful patterns emerge. Organize the materials by color, shape, texture. Simple classifications can be introduced: herbivorous, carnivorous animals; land dwellers, water dwellers; evergreen, deciduous trees, etc. If your child's interest warrants, proceed to study the class, order, and family distinctions. Science is systemized knowledge and it is necessary that classification follow observation.

As the child approaches 6 he is capable of learning to handle and care for the tools of science. The thermometer is probably the first instrument he encounters: the fever thermometer, the weather thermometer, and several more types in the kitchen. If he is interested in numbers, he can be taught to use a thermometer as well as to treat it with respect. A ruler, too, holds many possibilities for learning. The science of optics is open to our youngest child. The 3 year old can use and enjoy a magnifying glass, transparent colors, a simple periscope, the kaleidoscope, and he will quickly appreciate the need for an unscratched, unbroken lens. The child is prepared for such time as the parent may feel it is appropriate to introduce a telescope, a microscope, or field glasses.

Materials which can be adapted to these objectives are available in many inexpensive forms. If you can not find inset puzzles of a flower, a leaf, a bird, or a dinosaur, make them at home by pasting a picture on cardboard and cutting it into appropriate pieces. Paperbacks or sets of flashcards are available with pictures of birds, fish, flowers, insects, prehistoric animals, reptiles, rocks, trees. Look for them among materials for the older child; your pre-schooler is most willing to ignore the text until he is ready for it.

There is a wealth of diagrams and information in the dictionary as well as in the encyclopedia. A Scout Handbook is a good source book for suggestions on continuing your investigations as well as for background information. Seed catalogs make a most attractive text of flowers and vegetables. You can make scrapbooks, elaborate or simple, of classified pictures with their correct names. Your child will enjoy helping to cut and paste.

When the child is prepared to see variations in detail for himself, use real materials as much as possible. Walk with your child, sit, observe, taste, and feel. Books and pictures are better than nothing, but they do not replace experience. Visit the aquarium, the botanical gardens, the zoo, a farm, a bird sanctuary, a greenhouse, the museum of natural history. Use whatever facilities are available to you. Remember activity must form part of learning.

MEASURE AND NUMBER

Why must we feel like such revolutionaries? We have only a simple statement to make: the normal mother can teach her child to count from one to ten! Almost all the rest of the number work rests on this simple foundation. So that is our first desire—to encourage parents to teach this simple counting.

As you read the following Montessori ways of teaching numbers, remember that the mother may revise freely, *if* she understands the goal and sees a more suitable way to reach it. For example, some older children were picking up nails with a magnet. They tried to see how many nails could be hung one below the other. Four was a good score. Later, a child barely three years old took over the game and suddenly announced that she had six nails hanging. Not quite believing, the mother went to see. There were indeed six nails, and this had required considerable dexterity. As the usual way of learning to count, this would hardly be proposed as an exercise. But it would be silly to act as if this same child still needed solemn lessons according to the three steps of Seguin on the meaning of four, five, six. There is no substitute for observation.

Counting may be begun with the fingers if one great caution is observed. It is confusing to hold up five fingers, point to one of them and say one, then point to another and say two, etc. The confusion is increased if different fingers are sometimes called one and two. The solution is to hold up only one finger—any finger—and say one. Then hold up any two fingers and say two. Do this for each number. Test the child using Seguin's steps. If this caution is observed, there will be no lack of "materials" for learning to count up to ten. After that, many everyday things may be counted, such as stairs, trees, table-setting, shoes, or blocks.

Montessori offered the spindle boxes for counting. They make a self-correcting, repetitive exercise that the child can do alone. A box with ten divisions is marked with numerals from zero to nine, one for each division. No spindles are placed in the first section, one in the next, then two, etc. When nine spindles are placed in the last section, none of the original forty-five remain. If a mistake has been made, the child knows that he does not have the correct amount for the last section and must look for his mistake. A suitable substitute is to provide a divided box (an egg box?) with numbered sections. The child is to put into each section as many items as called for. They may be pegs or beans or beads. Later, provide cardboard cards with numbers. The child puts the numbers next to the sections of the box. Or let him arrange these numbers in a row. This shows whether he knows the correct order. Under each figure he may then place the appropriate number of items. If he is given only forty-five items to distribute, he will have just enough for the numbers one to nine and there will be some measure of self-correction.

The Montessori number materials have been devised with great ingenuity and teach many things that were not obvious at the first glance. Therefore, in spite of the remarks above about magnets and fingers we think that the special materials or close substitutes should be used whenever possible. The fascinating Montessori cylinders are the first exercise in learning gradation of size. The pink tower, broad stair, and number rods could be considered graphs. They serve to emphasize the relationship between number and measure, and in a very tangible way they provide remote preparation for a good deal of mathematics.

Looking at the pink tower, (see p. 39), one may make several observations. The parent may decide whether to teach the words involved, but he should know them.

1. The diameter of the cubes progresses evenly from one to ten. This is arithmetic progression. It may be drawn on a graph as a straight line.
2. The surface area of one face of the cubes progresses from one square centimeter to 4, to 9, to 16, and on to the square of ten. (Graph 1.)

3. The second cube is four times the first in surface area of one face, the third is 2.25 times the second,
the fourth is 1.77 times the third,
the fifth is 1.56 times the fourth,
the sixth is 1.44 times the fifth,
the seventh is 1.36 times the sixth,
the eighth is 1.31 times the seventh,
the ninth is 1.27 times the eighth,
the tenth is 1.24 times the ninth.

The ratio steadily diminishes, approaching but never reaching one. Though the child most certainly is not going to do any of this division to several decimal places, he does have a reasonable foundation for learning the idea of mathematical limits, just from looking at the cubes which make up the pink tower. (Graph 2.)

4. The change in the volume of the cubes is even more startling, progressing with increasing rapidity from one cubic centimeter to 8, to 27, to 64, to 125, and so on. (Graph 3.) This lesson can be reinforced by using many small cubes to build 1^3, 2^3, 3^3, 4^3, and so on. Graph 4 shows the ratios of these successive cubes.

However formidable our graphs may seem to parents, it is our firm belief that the children see the *idea* of the graphs by being able to see the pink tower day after day. We have no proof, but we think it likely that if the child's education continued consistently, he would not be puzzled when the time came to make or to read such graphs. Let any parent look at the startling change between the first and second cubes and the very slight difference between the two largest ones, to see for himself if this faith does not seem reasonable. This is why the pink tower is superior to any set of blocks with indefinite measurements and a chaos of pretty pictures on all sides. A substitute should be precisely measured. This is remote preparation for real mathematics.

Let us get back to the child's work. He learns to build the tower precisely. He may center each block. He may build steps, with one side of the tower straight, and then "walk" the smallest cube up the steps, learning that something plus one equals the next number.

The association of number and measure continues with the use of the broad stair and long stair, described in the chapter on didactic materials.

The number rods are introduced a few at a time, starting with the smallest three, using the steps of Seguin. This should take about a week for the average three year old. The child undoubtedly has had previous experience with two shoes, five fingers, perhaps eight raisins, or even six nails on a magnet. The number rods have other uses, however. After they are known by name they may be used for beginning addition:

1. Lay out the ten rod. Parallel to it put the nine rod. Then find the rod that can be added to the nine to equal the ten. Put the eight next to the two "tens" and find what is needed to make it equal. This way of arranging the rods may have been done previously with the long

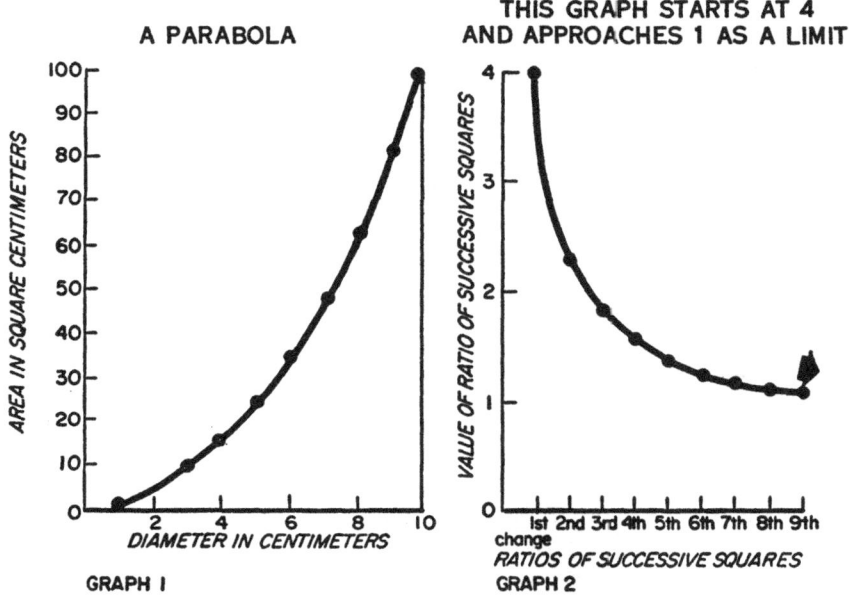

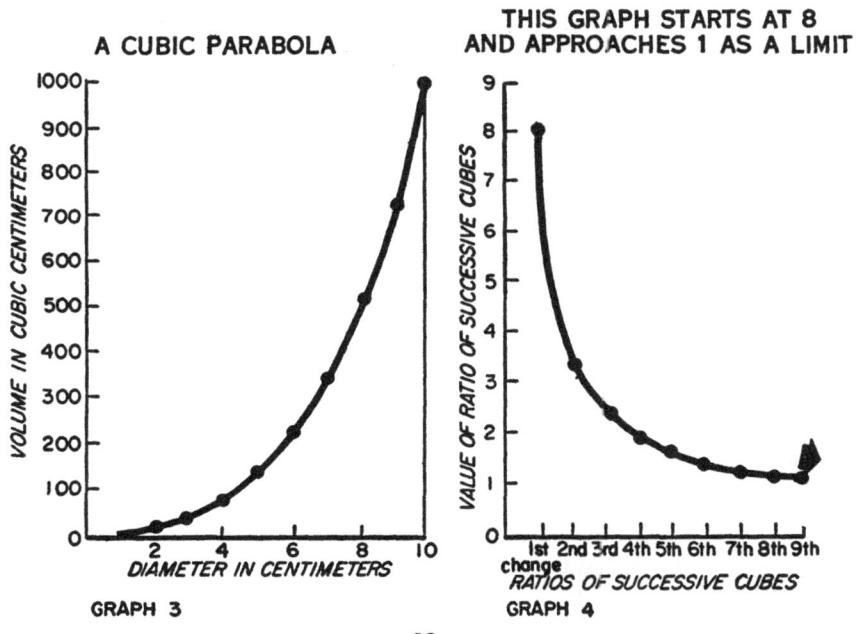

stairs, but now it is done using the names of the rods and it soon seems natural to say that nine and one are ten, eight and two are ten, etc.
2. Starting with the nine rod, arrange the other rods to make sums equal to nine.
3. Continue with eight and seven, and so forth.

The child who is using the number rods has probably learned the sandpaper letters. It is time for the sandpaper numbers. He traces each shape and names it, as described for learning letters. Then he may stand the sandpaper number beside the corresponding number rod, as is shown in some of Montessori's books. When he has learned to do the addition described above, the sandpaper numbers resting against the rods will be a written description of the adding that has been done.

The child may now be taught the meaning of odd and even. He sets out the cards from one to nine. He puts something like buttons under each card. These buttons or counters are arranged in columns of pairs for the even numbers and in columns of pairs plus one left over for the odd numbers. This is very simple, but it prevents confusion over a very simple concept.

Next there is proposed a memory game that is the beginning of the decimal system:
1. Let the child take a slip with a number on it from a basket. He is to go somewhere and get that many of something (blocks, toy cars, crayons, sticks, dandelions, etc.).
2. The mother must have some equivalent of the golden beads so that she has units, tens, hundreds, and thousands. Some mothers have strung together beads. Others have considered sewing very small glass beads to cards. One solution was to use a special adhesive paper in a design that was small and repetitive, so that it was easy to fasten it to cardboard and then to cut it into squares of one, strips of ten, and large squares of hundred. A long strip of this could be folded into ten squares so that there would be a thousand of manageable size. The memory game is played again. The child goes to the box and gets 5 "thousands" or 3 "hundreds" or 7 units.

After the child has mastered zero to ten using the number rods and sand letters, writing higher numbers may begin. For this there should be a supply of cards cut into four sizes. One could start with 5 x 8 index cards. Some would be cut into strips of 5 x 2. These would be numbered from zero to nine. Other cards would be cut to size 5 x 4. These would be numbered from ten to ninety, with the digits so spaced that the zero would be covered by one of the 5 x 2 cards. Cards cut 5 x 6 would be numbered from 100 to 900, and the full size cards would be numbered 1000 to 9000. Montessori classroom cards would be white, with green ink used for units and thousands, blue for tens, and red for hundreds. The colors of the cards could be changed instead, using any combination that seems attractive, and using a special marking pencil to make clear, legible writing. The cards are laid on top of each other to make such numbers as 4769.

At first the child calls the cards thousands, hundreds, tens (units he already knew from rods and sand numbers). The three steps of Seguin can be used to make the transition from "three tens" to "thirty."

Now the child may play a game that begins like the memory game. The parent says, "Would you get 3 hundreds?" or 4 thousands, or 6 tens. "Now would you get the card for 3 hundred?" or 4 thousands or 6 tens. Several numbers may be laid out, in beads and in cards.

One fine day, after several numbers have been laid out, the parent says, "Let's count all the beads." So they count the units and find a number card to match. They count the tens and find the card. They count the hundreds and find the card, slipping the ten half under the unit, and the hundred half under the ten so that the number looks right. They count the thousands, find the card, and put it in its place. (The parent should have the foresight to avoid a problem with "carrying" the first time this is done.) Now he may say, if he likes, "This is called addition." It is our experience that a four year old found great pleasure in setting up numbers and adding them.

After a little practice or when the child makes it necessary by setting up large numbers, the parent may demonstrate "carrying." It is very simple. If he has ten units, he carries them to the bank and changes them to a ten. If he has ten tens, he carries them to the bank and changes them to a hundred. He changes ten hundreds to a thousand. The carrying is done with the beads, before the number card is found. This paragraph is short, but the lessons may take weeks.

The child has presumably been learning penmanship in the meantime, and when it seems suitable, he may substitute writing for the cards.

To demonstrate subtraction a number is set up with the beads and cards. The number to be taken away is set up with cards only. Then that many beads are taken from the first number. The remainder is counted and the number written by card. "Borrowing" is done when necessary by changing the thousands into hundreds, hundreds into tens, etc.

Our experience in multiplication only includes construction of the multiplication tables. Multiplication is said to be only repeated addition. This is easy for multiplying by 3 or 4, but not entirely helpful if the multiplier is to be 697.

Multiplication tables are constructed by having pegboards and pegs or else piles of something such as dried beans. For example, four pegs might be put in a row and then counted and the answer written: $4 \times 1 = 4$. Then two rows of four pegs each would be set up and counted and the answer written neatly below the previous answer: $4 \times 2 = 8$. Then three rows are prepared, etc. These tables are constructed and written with the usual Montessorian opportunity for repetition so that the child has time to learn and be sure of himself.

For fun, we made up our own "Montessori materials" to teach the idea of the binary system. To write the numbers up to one hundred, make a hundred small cards (3 x 5 index cards cut in quarters would be good) which say nothing on one side and 1 on the other. This is Set A. Make another hundred cards with one side nothing, the other side 2. This is Set

B. Another hundred will be nothing or 4 (Set C). The next hundred will be nothing or 8 (Set D). Other sets will be 16 or nothing (Set E), 32 or nothing (Set F), and 64 or nothing (Set G).

To replace the place-value of units, tens, hundreds, thousands, we now have our seven sets, equal to 2^0, 2^1, 2^2, 2^3, 2^4, 2^5, 2^6. The parent may imitate our diagram, and the child will quickly imitate the parent. In each column there are only two choices—one side or the other of the cards. This is what binary means. We have written 14 as 8 4 2 0 for clarity, though many would have written 1 1 1 0, which is very confusing until one has the clue. (See p. 33.)

HISTORY

An understanding of history is based on the comprehension of two concepts: time and change. At birth, the infant is only aware of the present. With mental development the child learns to distinguish the present from the past, to understand that today followed yesterday. This ability to judge time is the first step towards an awareness of what is history.

Change, the second concept, is the distinguishing feature between past and present. Change involves movement: action and reaction; cause and effect. Movement, one could say, is the subject matter of history while time is the convenient outline of or method for dividing the subject matter. An understanding of both concepts, therefore, must precede the actual accumulation of historical knowledge.

Once these concepts are known to the child, history becomes a natural subject for his curiosity. His first topics of research are related to his immediate environment; he learns of the past, indirectly, by questioning the why and how of his present, and the success of this oral research is proportionate to the interest and patience of his parents. Showing family photographs, recalling earlier incidents, preparing a weekly schedule or monthly calendar are some methods which illustrate the past of his immediate environment. History, at this level, helps the child to self-possession, to understanding himself as a member of twentieth-century society.

When the child is able to read, his historical interests are no longer limited to objects in his immediate environment. He can now gain direct knowledge of the past through individual inquiry and discovery. But, as during the years when the child gave order to his information by relating newly acquired data to his present world, he must now establish meaning through a new pattern of association: he must understand the relationship between past events which are not part of his environment. He does this by arranging his historical data in a chronological sequence.

One visual aid which helps the child to establish chronological relationship is a time-line. Constructed from a roll of paper or pieces of cardboard laid side by side, the time-line is marked into centuries, dating from 2000 B.C. to 2000 A.D., noting the birth of Christ as the central point from which our time is labeled. Along this chronological device, the child can trace topical development. One Montessori exercise is to place cards, which picture and date various stages in the history of such topics as transportation, houses,

The Arabic Numerals	2^6 =64	2^5 =32	2^4 =16	2^3 =8	2^2 =4	2^1 =2	2^0 =1
0							0
1							1
2						2	0
3						2	1
4					4	0	0
5					4	0	1
6					4	2	0
7					4	2	1
8				8	0	0	0
9				8	0	0	1
10				8	0	2	0
11				8	0	2	1
12				8	4	0	0
13				8	4	0	1
14				8	4	2	0
15				8	4	2	1
16			16	0	0	0	0
17			16	0	0	0	1
18			16	0	0	2	0

30	0	0	16	8	4	2	1
31	0	0	16	8	4	2	0
32	0	32	0	0	0	0	1
33	0	32	0	0	0	0	1
34	0	32	0	0	0	2	1

62	0	32	16	8	4	2	0
63	0	32	16	8	4	2	1
64	64	0	0	0	0	0	1
65	64	0	0	0	0	0	1
66	64	0	0	0	0	2	0
67	64	0	0	0	0	2	1
68	64	0	0	0	4	0	0

or dress, on the time-line at the section representing the appropriate century. The child can then measure the time and change involved in the progress of such objects from stage to stage. For another exercise, using his own time-line, the child might copy various historical facts in the proper spaces. Thus, he can visualize the chronological relationship between numerous events, as well as the gradual development of a specific topic. The uses of this educational tool are numerous.

The purpose of the time-line is to help the child organize the knowledge which he has acquired from various sources. Reading is, of course, the most direct source for historical facts. More tangible objects, however, have much value for the child. Collections of stamps, coins, maps, flags, as well as the celebration of national holidays, can stimulate a child's natural interest in the past. The traditions of Thanksgiving Day, for example, should lead to enlightenment concerning the Colonial period of American history; Independence Day festivities to the Revolutionary period.

History is a social discipline which will both expand a child's interests and help him to organize his discoveries. The subject is a prepared pathway to culture along which a child can run, walk at a steady pace, or stoop often to examine particularly interesting stones. It is, essentially, an individual endeavor which gives increasing enjoyment from childhood to adulthood.

ART

Children see and respond to beauty. In this increasingly urbanized world where the only wildflowers a child may know are dandelions poking through gravel, there is almost a need to see underlying beauty as well as the obvious. The sensitivity of the child is there, only the beginning skills have to be taught. Art teachers with wide experience with children tell us that every child can learn to draw, just as he can learn how to read or to subtract. The big differences are (1) that children are conditioned to think immediately of drawing as fun, and (2) that parents are often afraid to teach children to draw if they themselves do not know how. But even parents who cannot draw the proverbial straight line *can* teach their children to draw.

The parent who teaches his child to see as an artist sees, and to try to draw what he sees, not only trains the intellect and the hand to work together, but enriches the entire world of his child.

Some Montessori Ideas on Teaching

Maria Montessori sought always to provide in the education of the child two things: freedom and a sense of reality. These basic ideas should underlie all efforts of a parent who is teaching his child to draw.

Dr. Montessori believed that the years between three and six are crucial for the construction of the ability to make a free choice. How can the young artist be led to exercise true freedom? He can be taught to make a horse look like a horse, or a tree like a tree, and yet be encouraged to place his house or his tree wherever he chooses, if he chooses to draw it at all. Teach him how to draw, but grant the "artist" his subject.

Children generally are deeply engrossed in their work as they draw. But whenever one breaks his concentration to ask for instruction, the parent can help. The best way to help is to show the child carefully how a particular object may be drawn, rather than suggesting he work it out by himself. At each step of the way, a parent can be alert for special problems and isolate these, teaching the solution step by step.

As in all other aspects of a child's growth, there are stages which are particularly ripe for teaching the discipline of drawing. The child himself can lead the way, letting the parent know when he is ready for further work in copying, or sketching, or the use of color. The exact age of acquiring a particular ability will depend upon when the child is first introduced to art materials. The proper age for introducing art materials might well be whenever the mother and child see eye to eye on their use. The atmosphere of calm which Maria Montessori so loved is not possible when a one and one-half year old uses crayons to write on walls and the mother becomes upset.

Teaching a child to draw accurately appeals to his sense of reality. A small child can be highly critical of his own work or that of other children if it doesn't look like what it was meant to be. A child *wants* to be precise and *prefers* to have the house he has drawn look like a house. Maria Montessori pointed out that the child looks outward and sees reality—sometimes with an exactness of detail which would astound an adult. You have surely heard a small child comment on an obscure detail of a magazine picture.

Art Tools in the Home

Before looking around the home for tools for the home art course, some parents might want to take a second look at the one tool that is imported into almost every home—the coloring book. A coloring book means exactly what it says to most parents—a book to color, a book to teach the child how to color. But the child sees more than the colors. He sees and records in his absorbent mind all the lines and shapes as well. Pictures that are distorted do not help a child to learn to draw. Unfortunately, all too many coloring books available today are in this category.

The Montessori axiom of having self-correction built into the teaching materials is suggested in the coloring books where the picture is already colored on one page and blank on the opposite page. The child can color the outlined figure and see for himself that a green face is not as close to reality as a green jacket. Discipline is provided in the material itself. Coloring books are appropriately used during the ages of $2\frac{1}{2}$ to 6 when the child's sense of color is being refined.

When teaching a child to draw, the first home tool to consider is a mirror. A child can be taught to try to draw what he sees of himself in a mirror. A full length mirror is best of all for it teaches the proportions of the entire body. After enough sessions of drawing self-portraits, the child knows with his hand and his eye—although he probably can't verbalize it—that his head is 1/8 of his body, that his eyes are right in the middle of his head, that his nose is halfway between his eyebrows and the bottom of his chin. It takes practice and time to acquire such knowledge, but the rules are being learned at each drawing session. An artist will point out that an image is seen more clearly in a mirror than with the naked eye since tricks of light can distort what the eye sees.

Another way of making the child aware of his own size and shape is to have him lie down on a large piece of wrapping paper while his parent traces around him. The child can then color his outline and learn that his skin tone is a mixture of red and yellow. From here it is just one step more to learn that most skin tones are a combination of red and yellow in varying degrees of each, and to acquire, through this knowledge, a better understanding of the sameness of all peoples.

A helpful home tool for teaching art is the windowpane, which is very useful as a sketching sheet. Using a crayon on the pane of glass, the child can be shown how to trace with exactness the world of reality that he sees outside. Perspective, the shape of a tree trunk, the reach of a branch can be learned this way. This procedure is a means of learning accuracy, of training the hand not to distort nature. A particular window or two might be set apart for this phase of the art lessons, and a commercial window cleaning product plus a little rubbing will restore the window's sparkle when the lesson is over.

The use of tracing paper can also increase a child's accuracy in drawing. Tracing a half dozen butterflies out of the encyclopedia, for example, will teach the child what a butterfly looks like, and when the later day comes that he wants to paint or sketch one in a composition of his own, the groundwork will already have been done. The child can acquire a visual vocabulary through such tracing sessions. It is hard to think of a more self-correcting art material than a sheet of tracing paper.

Surrounding the child with beauty may be considered as preparing an environment for the child artist. Children are acutely aware of the use of color in the home. They are conscious of the appearance of a meal, of the colors of the food on the plate. A bowl of flowers seldom goes unnoticed. Beauty beyond the usual scope of the eye can be introduced through use of a magnifying glass. In order to draw a leaf well, a child must know its skeleton; a leaf structure is easier to learn—and much more exciting to observe—through a magnifying glass.

The child should always be encouraged to feel that he *can* learn how to draw, that it is exciting to draw, and that perhaps by the time he is six he will be able to illustrate his own stories. Of couse, the child should also have an abundance of free play with paper, crayon, paint, clay, and other art materials.

THE USE OF THE DIDACTIC MATERIALS

Doctor Montessori was concerned most with what she called the child's "formative period," which is from three to seven years of age. For this age group she provided a special environment. It was a children's house, the *Casa dei Bambini,* a real house but with furnishings small enough to fit the child. It had a garden and play area outside. Inside, there were plants in every room and each child had his own plant to care for and watch grow. On the walls were pictures of children, families, landscapes, flowers, fruits, and scenes of biblical and historical events. Games, picture albums, and geometric solids were provided on the tables in the living room. Here, also, children played small harps, a piano, or other musical instruments. In the dining room the children set the table, carrying trays of china, glasses, and food. The teaching materials were kept in a central room called the intellectual room. The children felt a responsibility for this special home and took great delight in taking care of it.

Many of the features of Montessori's *Casa dei Bambini* are naturally provided in the well-arranged home, and parents can make use of most of the teaching methods practiced there. Practical life exercises such as opening doors, sweeping floors, wiping tables are taught by having the mother perform the chore in which the child indicates interest. She should do this very slowly and precisely so that repetition is possible.

At the *Casa dei Bambini,* the order and pace at which the teaching materials were presented to each child were geared to his natural development. Teaching was accomplished mainly through demonstration, the precise actions of the teacher providing a model for the children to imitate. The teacher tried to avoid correcting the child, but was ready to guide him if needed. The teaching materials were designed to allow the child to find and correct his own errors as he learned by doing. The didactic materials gave attention to three areas of learning:

1. *Motor Education.* The child learned to control his movements, and to use his hands and fingers more skillfully.
2. *Sensory Education.* The child sharpened his ability to observe differences and similarities in what he saw, heard, felt, tasted, and smelled.
3. *Language Education.* The child learned to associate what he saw with the appropriate spoken word for the object or concept, and developed the basic skills leading toward writing and reading.

The same equipment and even the same exercises can contribute to all three types of education. The Montessori didactic materials are described in this chapter. Properly used, they lay a secure foundation for the development of the child's muscles and senses.

Motor Education

The aim of muscular or motor education is to bring order to the child's movements. The primary movements of everyday life are included in the muscular education. The care of the person, help in the household, gardening, manual work, gymnastic exercise, and rhythmic movements should be given attention.

Frames for **buttoning, lacing,** etc., are helpful for learning to dress and undress. It should be remembered, however, that the primary purpose of the frames is to develop muscular coordination and to strengthen the child's fingers. The method of using the frames is typical of the Montessori way.

The parent should sit by the child, performing the necessary movements very precisely and slowly, separating the movements into parts, and showing them plainly. Such frames are easy to make. At home it will even seem natural to use clothing.

One of the gymnastic exercises is *walking on a line* without stepping off. A line can be drawn with chalk or paint, or the many lines around us (curbs, walks, etc.) can be used. After the children learn to walk slowly on the line, a rhythmic exercise can be added. A simple march can be played or sung while the children are walking. A balance exercise can be used. The children can carry full containers without spilling contents, carry bells without having them ring, or hold a flag straight without swerving from the line. Ladders are useful for balancing exercises. They may be placed flat on the ground or slightly raised. Gym sets are obviously helpful.

Sensory Education

The parent should follow a definite order in educating the child's senses: (1) recognition of identities; (2) recognition of contrasts; and (3) discrimination between objects very similar. First the parent has the child pair objects. Then he presents the extremes of a series of objects. Last of all, the child learns to observe differences even when the similarities outweigh the contrast.

After the child learns to compare a series of objects and recognizes the quality that differs, then—and only then—the parent fixes the idea of this quality with a word. "This is long. This is short." This naming is the first step of Seguin. Then the child is asked to point to the object. "Which is long? Which is short?" This pointing is the second step of Seguin. Finally, the child pronounces the name of the quality when the parent asks, "What is this? What is that?" This identification is the third step of Seguin.

The terms used must be exact. For example, "small" should not be called "thin;" "dimensions" should not be called "forms." To get the child's attention concentrated on the particular sensory stimulus that is being taught, the parent may remove other articles around the area. The parent should always familiarize himself with the material before giving it to the child. He must observe the child. At times the parent may have to hold or guide his hand. The parent should try not to let the child risk failure until he has a reasonable chance of success.

The first formal sensory exercises for the two and one-half to three year old child are four sets of *cylindrical insets*. They are four solid pieces of wood, in each of which is inserted a row of ten cylinders, each of which has a knob for a handle. In the first series the height of the cylinders is constant and the diameter varies; in the second, the cylinders vary in height and the diameter is constant; in the third, the height increases while the diameter decreases; in the fourth, both height and diameter increase together.

The usual Montessori procedure is employed when the child is first introduced to the cylindrical insets. The parent should demonstrate completely the necessary motions, taking the cylinders out of the holes, mixing them, and replacing them. Then the child attempts to repeat these actions. If he has difficulty in getting a cylinder back into the correct hole, the parent shows him that by feeling the cylinder and the holes he may be more successful. The sense of touch is more highly developed than the sense of sight in the very young.

After having some practice with the cylindrical insets, the child is shown how to use some other materials. When a new exercise is introduced the old ones are not taken away. Often a child likes to return to the old ones to review what he has learned.

The *pink tower* is a series of ten wooden blocks the sides of which increase from one centimeter to ten centimeters. The child builds a tower using the biggest block first, then the next biggest, and so on. When the tower is built, he takes it down and rebuilds. To develop poise, the child can learn to carry the tower without toppling it.

The *broad stairs* are a set of rectangular brown blocks, decreasing in height and width, length being constant. All are twenty centimeters long, but the square cross section diminishes from ten centimeters a side for the thickest one to one centimeter a side for the thinnest. The child begins with the thinnest or thickest and then places the rest in order forming stairs.

The *long stairs* differ in length only. Each is four centimeters square in cross section, but they vary in length from ten centimeters to one meter. The child compares and arranges the rods according to length, giving the appearance of stairs seen from the side. The *number rods* are like the long stairs in size but these rods are used to illustrate addition and subtraction. At home the number rods can serve both purposes.

The exercises using the pink tower, broad stairs, long stairs, and number rods might seem easier than using the cylindrical insets, but they are not. When using the cylindrical insets the child is guided by touch, and the equipment is self-corrective. The child does not have these aids when making judgments required by the exercises just described.

The next material to be introduced is a *rough and smooth sandpaper board*. This is a rectangle, half smooth, half covered with sandpaper. The child's fingers should be washed before a lesson to make the finger tips more responsive. The tips of the index and the middle fingers of the child's dominant hand touch the board lightly as they move across from left to right, the child saying "rough" or "smooth" as appropriate. At first the child sees the board, but later he may be blindfolded. Later still he rubs the board with a piece of wood to identify roughness and smoothness by sound and touch. This, too, may be done blindfolded. At a later stage, pairs of boards with different degrees of roughness can be used for identification and matching by touch.

Next a set of *pairs of fabrics* can be used to develop further the tactile sense. The child learns the fabrics and then identifies and matches them blindfolded. Silk and velvet may be used as the first contrasting materials; then other fabrics are introduced. Another tactile exercise is having the blindfolded child identify objects that are familiar to him. To entertain a child with measles, one parent collected at least fifty small items from around the house and put them under the top blanket. The child gleefully identified everything.

To refine the sense of *color*, two *boxes* each containing duplicate sets of sixty-four colored tablets are used. There are eight main colors (red, orange, yellow, green, blue, violet, brown, gray) and eight shades of each color. The child is shown two contrasting colors such as red and blue. Then he is gradually presented with the other main colors. When he masters this much, he is given the different shades of each hue ranging from dark to light. To help the child differentiate between the hues, the parent has him pick the darkest and then the lightest shade of each color. After he can identify and match these two extremes, his accuracy increases and he is able to grade the other shades. Some children become so proficient in this sensory exercise that they develop a "color memory." That is, they can look at a certain shade, go into another room, and pick the same shade from a pile of colors. When spools of thread are used for the exercise, the child is taught to handle them by the top or bottom of the spool to avoid touching the thread. Wool, paint samples, colored tile, or other materials may be used, and it is not essential to have 64 different shades. After the child has learned the colors, the parent can call attention to their presence in ordinary objects in the environment.

The *geometric cabinet* has six drawers containing thirty-six square wooden frames, each of which has a large geometrical inset in the center. Each inset has a small knob-like handle. The first drawer contains a circle, a square, a triangle, and three blanks. The six insets in the second drawer are circles decreasing in diameter. The third set of insets is a square and five rectangles whose lengths are equal to the sides of the square while the widths gradually decrease. Next come six different triangles—equilateral, isosceles, scalene, right angle, obtuse angle, and acute angle. The next insets are six polygons having five to ten sides. The last drawer has insets of oval, ellipse, rhombus, trapezoid, and flower forms.

A wooden frame is used with this material. The first insets used in the frame are the circle, triangle, and square. Again the child is taught to aid his sight by touch. While he holds the inset by the knob with his subdominant hand, he feels the outline of the inset and the corresponding aperture in the frame with the tips of the index and middle fingers of the dominant hand. He moves his fingers in the direction of writing, left to right. Then he inserts the inset in its corresponding opening. After he knows the difference among these forms he learns their names. When he is able to replace these first forms correctly, he is given two triangles and two circles of different sizes. Soon he will be able to insert all six circles and triangles in their places. Gradually the rest of the forms are given to the child. When he knows the insets and how to replace them, he does the exercise blindfolded.

After the final mastery of the insets, the child is given three series of white cards on which are figures identical to the insets. In the first series, the figures are cut out of colored paper and mounted on the cards; in the second, the figures are heavy line drawings; and in the third, the figures are represented only by a thin line. The child mixes up six or eight of these cards from the first series and six or eight corresponding insets. He puts the insets on the matching cards. Here he does not have the sense of touch to guide him. Thus, he learns gradually the meaning of the line, passing from the solid form to the form merely drawn in outline. He acquires an idea of symbolism. He will come to understand how a series of lines can stand for an object. The child continues this exercise using the other two sets of cards.

Later on the child will be shown the *solid geometrical forms*. These are the sphere, cylinder, cone, prism, pyramid, and the regular polyhedrons: tetrahedron, octahedron, cube, dodecahedron, and icosahedron. (These may be made from cardboard, or from science kits.) Montessori suggests using their motions to illustrate some of their characteristics. Show how the sphere rolls in every direction, the cylinder rolls in one direction only, the cone rolls around its point, the prism and the pyramid stand still but the prism falls over more easily than the pyramid.

To sharpen the auditory sense, *sound boxes* are used. These are two identical sets of six closed cardboard cylinders. They are filled with different substances, such as gravel or sand, to produce different sounds when shaken. The sounds vary from loud to almost imperceptible. The exercises consist of recognizing similar sounds and comparing different sounds. Covered fliptop cigarette boxes, small salt shakers, and opaque containers of any type may be used.

The sense of weight differences is made more acute by use of the *weight tablets*. Of identical size, these tablets are made of wood of different densities such as lignum vitae (a very heavy wood), oak, and basswood. Duplicate sets of three tablets are provided. The child rests a tablet delicately on the inner surface of his four fingers, moving his hand up and down to feel the weight. In this manner he matches the tablets and arranges them in order of weight. After the child has been initiated into the exercise by the parent, he repeats it blindfolded. When he takes off the blindfold he can see by the natural color of the pieces of wood if he has arranged the tablets correctly. In addition to developing the sense of weight, this exercise helps develop delicate movements of the hand, since the child strives to make the weighing movements as imperceptible as possible.

To develop discrimination in temperature, the child can use cups or glasses filled with graded mixtures of hot and cold water.

Metal bells help to develop the sense of pitch. They stand upon wooden rectangular bases and are alike in appearance. Each of two duplicate sets forms an octave. One set is prearranged according to the scale. With a small hammer, the child strikes the first note of the series already arranged. Then from among a second series of bells the child tries to find the same sound. He continues until he has paired all the notes of the scale. Next the child strikes in rapid succession the bells that are already arranged, accompanying the sound with his voice. Eventually, from a set not arranged in order of pitch, he will be able to find and arrange each note of the scale. Montessori also used resonant metal tubes, small harps, and pianos for developing the sense of pitch. Here differences in timbre come to be perceived together with the differences in tone.

To improve the child's attention to sound there is a most important exercise, not in producing, but in eliminating all noise. It is the *lesson of silence*. First, have the child find a comfortable position. He closes his eyes. The parent tells the child not to move. Then comes a silence. Slight sounds such as the ticking of the clock or the chirping of birds, which were unnoticed before, are now heard. This listening exercise can arise spontaneously when walking in the woods or along the beach, at night in bed, or in any new or familiar environment. The lesson of silence helps the child to develop self-control as it prepares him to follow more accurately the sounds of spoken language.

The sense of smell may be developed by filling pairs of small containers such as salt shakers with different fragrant substances.

These special exercises of attention, observation, comparison and classification have helped the child to form ideas of quantity, identity, differences, and gradation which form the basis of all calculation. Now he is ready for direct preparation for writing, reading and numbers—at about four years of age.

FOREIGN LANGUAGES

Learning to speak is one of the first intellectual tasks confronting the infant. It is a difficult job, but one for which the child is well prepared.

Observation shows that children have a special sensitivity to language during their first six years. We may teach the child *what* to speak, but he teaches himself *how*. He learns his mother-tongue, unaware of the complexity of its grammar or its difficulties in pronunciation. It comes naturally to him, through daily usage, backed up by his motivation to communicate.

During this sensitive period, a second language can be introduced to the child. The same precision should be used as in teaching him to speak his mother tongue. He should hear careful speech; the pronunciation should be clear; the grammar should be correct.

The ideal way in which to help a child absorb a second language is to be yourselves bilingual parents, and to use both languages in the home. Few children are so lucky in this regard, of course. But there are a number of alternatives available.

If no one at home can speak another language, parents might arrange for the child to hear and converse with relatives or neighbors—or even a tutor—who can.

Language teaching records are available from most public libraries, as are records of songs in other languages. Educational television stations offer language lessons on several levels of difficulty. These can assist a parent who would like to help his child, but whose high school French needs refreshing.

The sensitive period for language is the time of golden opportunity for learning with ease. Languages may still be learned after this period is over, of course. Yet, as high school students and adults attest, it will later take a conscientious effort to acquire this knowledge which comes so readily to the small child.

SOME PERSONAL EXPERIENCES

I

An Eighteen Month Old Baby

Although the following observations developed on a day to day basis, I feel it is the end results that give meaning and practical application to what Dr. Montessori meant when she advocated that the parent look to himself as well as to the child. There has been much trial and error in our experience, but here are our successes.

Area 1—Attitude of Parent

Through our 18 month old I came to know myself as I appeared to him. As early as ten months of age he reacted to my behavior. On days that I rushed through the household chores and blazed a hurried and confused trail behind me, he would cry with frustration and would attempt to follow me frantically. It was only later that I realized that his peace of mind was being shattered by the tension that my hurried attitude and quick voice created. As soon as I deliberately slowed my running gait to a quiet walk that he could keep up with, he was given the freedom to work at his own physical and mental growth in an atmosphere of peace and respect. Instead of making a mad dash to the ringing phone, I walked, and the extra ring never seemed to bother the caller. At times we even play the whisper game —he takes great delight in hearing my whispered tone of voice and has to lie quietly and be very still in order to hear what I am telling him.

I have discovered that "to be inviting and a joy to the child" requires time, restraint, and—more important—a great deal of thoughtfulness on the part of parents. Selfish habits have to be broken, but the end results are a rich reward for all concerned, for the child is being given the greatest gift of all— the opportunity to be himself.

Our walk to the store afforded another lesson in the area of parental attitude. Being 18 months old, our son wants to walk blocks and blocks (without holding his mother's hand) just for the sheer joy of walking. On the other hand, I have a goal, namely to get to the store and then home to resume chores that are awaiting me. It took terrific restraint in the beginning to redirect my desire to rush; instead, I let David walk joyfully at his own pace. When he became tired, he would sit for two or three minutes and then resume his exercise. It wasn't long before I realized that the walk took maybe ten minutes longer, but instead of seeming as if it were a two hour ordeal, it was in fact an enjoyable 30 minute walk. The work of walking was refreshing to David. It was my rushed attitude that tired him previously. I do want to insert that we have rules when we go walking, such as holding mother's hand when crossing the street—but they are accepted gladly because he is allowed to choose freely among other activities such as walking, resting, or stopping to discover a leaf or flower. He is too young to realize the consequences of running into a street, but just as there are rules in the adult's world, there must be rules for the child.

Area 2—Free Exercise of the Will

Since I have touched lightly on the subject of free choice within an ordered environment, I will give a few more examples of how we are trying to provide opportunities for our 18 month old to exercise his will at home.

Although verbal communication on David's part is in the process of being acquired, he has gained an understanding of the spoken word. When he was ten months we started to name objects and activities as: "David take a bath," "read a book," "I put on my shoes." Now at 18 months when we call to him, "Close the door, please," "Let's go take a bath," "Let's eat," "Let's go to bed," he runs gleefully to the said object or appropriate room and awaits our arrival. He is not obeying our command but practicing an activity of the intellect—namely, understanding the spoken language and taking joy in carrying out an idea. Going to bed simply means that we walk to the crib, but this is an activity that he knows he can do and for that reason alone he wants to do it. Just as he walks for the joy of walking, so too, does he carry out suggestions—because he understands. He is understanding for the joy of understanding. He realizes his limitations when it comes to executing all the activities involved in taking a bath, or getting ready for bed, but he does understand the concept and wants to exercise that much of his developed will. He has constructed his movements to do part of an activity for himself.

When David was a year old we started to guide his right hand in the art of holding a spoon correctly. To keep the lesson simple we used an empty dish; explanation was through demonstration only. When he became distracted, we dropped the activity for another day. By 18 months he showed the desire to feed himself and from the first bite he has held the spoon correctly. There was no frustration, for I let him tell me when he was ready seriously to feed himself and the previous spoon practice enabled him to direct food to his mouth without meeting failure. I also discovered that when he was tired and fussy at meal-time, an unusually soft spoken voice or the humming of a melody helped to relax him as well as keep me calm when the food spilled and his temper flared.

Being 18 months old, David frequently forgets where he has put a favorite toy. Sometimes he can call for help by naming the object as "truck" but other times frustration sets in because he is unable to express himself. I have found it most helpful and calming if, with as few words as possible, I give my hand to him and ask him to show me where it might be. Often he can't reach the desired object, so I will put it at an advantage point for him. By letting him show me the way and encouraging him whenever possible to pick up the fallen or lost article, I feel he is getting practice in acting for himself and in commanding himself.

Area 3—Reading

Reading has come to mean a very special activity in our house. We usually reserve the hour before bedtime for this quiet activity, although there have been many other occasions during the daytime when it has been used as a "quieting" activity. We started reading to David when he was ten months old and there were rules even at that time about the care of books. David was reminded gently but firmly that books were not to be bitten nor torn. Usually the adult's voice when reading, or the activity of pointing to the pictures or of turning the pages was enough distraction to get his attention back on the reading. Even when magazines were a fascination—as soon as I heard the first tear I would take five minutes to instill the idea that books are not to be torn and then we would leaf through the pages properly and look at the pictures. At 18 months David can be trusted with his books. They are worn from wear but not from abuse. He now asks for them frequently and either indicates that we read to him or he will imitate us by sitting in a chair as long as 15 minutes and reading quietly to himself in his own way. *Pat the Bunny* has been most popular for it makes use of the senses and David can do many of the exercises without relying on the spoken word of the adult.

Area 4—Muscle Coordination and Independence

At ten months David gave a strong indication that he wanted space in order to move about and to exercise. An hour a day for the first few weeks proved sufficient and was enormously successful. By the time he was a year he was spending a total of four hours a day exercising and investigating. He was intent on climbing furniture and stairs and closing every door in sight. The only time he received adult help was when the fingers got stuck in the door or he fell from a high place. For the most part he learned quickly from his own mistakes: his confidence and agility developed steadily. It meant I had to work at suppressing my fears and concern; I soon learned that when he fell he was relaxed, and a soft spoken word of encouragement had him upon his feet trying again.

By the time he was 14 months he was content to play in his playpen for an hour in the morning and an hour in the evening. Having worked most of the day at his large muscular development, he was ready for small muscle activity. The playpen represented the needed confined area to encourage quiet activity and he displayed real concentration rather than aimless play, i.e., playing with nuts and bolts or directing his truck to go a certain way. It marked the beginning of the hand and eye working together and to this day he spends hours directing an object on wheels to go in and out and up and under large objects. He does such activity with great deliberation and exactness. I let David tell me when he wanted to get out of the pen, and as a result he never objected to the confined area or times of quiet work.

Area 5—Prayer

At 15 months we introduced David to bedtime prayers. We have made it a practice to pray as if David in his own words were talking to God. The content of each prayer changes from day to day, corresponding with the day's activities and events. Although his understanding is still greatly limited, he does realize that prayer time is a special and quiet time. By establishing the habit of prayer as a real talking to God, rather than the thoughtless repeating of words, I am hopeful that he will learn how to truly lift his heart and mind to God.

II

A Four Year Old Child

To write about a Montessori experience now is difficult for me, because I have only recently discovered this approach to the child. Perhaps if I write of something that was not a Montessori experience, her ideals will stand out nevertheless.

Surely, in attempting to understand the child, and in preparing the environment most beneficial to children's development, parents, teachers, and scientists would like to find some "universal laws" about children. It seems to me that possibly Montessori's idea of "sensitive periods" in a child's life might be just such a law. I am hopeful that through understanding Montessori better, I will be able to learn to observe the child in such a way as to enable me to tell what kind of sensitive period the child is going through, and just how to prepare his environment in order that he may better "create himself."

Wishing to help the development of our daughter, I asked some experts, including the principal of a nearby public school, whether it was wise for parents to help their children learn the letters. Our daughter, then four years of age, was most interested. The principal suggested that I should enrich the child's life to the fullest—but not in the area of reading and writing.

A year and a half later, our daughter is in kindergarten. She has already voiced her feeling that writing is work, the kind of work that is a burden and thus best avoided. She is expected to print her name, although she has been given no instruction as to how to do it, nor background in phonetics, nor, in fact, in any kind of activity involving the alphabet. No wonder the writing of her name has become a burden to her!

Thus, a sensitive period was lost.

And thus, adults labor to attempt to teach children that which during a sensitive period, and with the adequate Montessori materials, the child can teach himself as part of his joy in living.

A FINAL WORD TO PART II

Our study could not be exhaustive. There are a few topics we would like to mention briefly.

We wish we had been competent to discuss early musical learning. Leopold Mozart should be remembered. The new Japanese system for teaching violin to young children is also indicative of future possibilities.

The exercises in pratical life, in care of oneself and of the environment, are important in early development. We think it a sufficient guide for the mother to remember that she is the magician whose hand is quicker than the child's eye. If he is to learn, she must slow down. This does not mean that her whole day is to be spent is slow-motion, but that from time to time when she thinks a child is interested she should do a particular job slowly enough so that he may imitate her. We do not think it is necessary to analyze every activity into thirty-eleven steps.

To learn the faithful performance of chores is not the same as learning a particular skill.

With regard to religion, all that Montessori said about the absorbent mind should be meditated upon. Furthermore, her remarks on language as the means of transmitting national and religious sentiment should be pondered. Daily words, acts, and attitudes during the child's early years must be considered in addition to more formal acts.

It is fervently to be hoped that those parents who read this pamphlet will not succumb to the sometimes over-whelming temptation to seek for carefully detailed lists of procedures in their own approach to Montessori in the home, but rather that they will heed the example of Montessori herself whose work proceeded according to a cyclical pattern, from hypothesis to experimentation to reformulation, and "Look at the child;" *this* child, in *this* family, in *these* circumstances at *this* time.

This pamphlet is based on the reading, discussion, and experience of a group of mothers. The authors are: Arynne Bermont, Ruth Brake, Adoria Brock, Margaret Clarke, Genevieve P. Connell, Iby Heller, Margaret Jackson, Sarah B. Jackson, Betty Levinson, Jean D. Linehan, Evelyn McQuie, Martha O'Keefe, Betty Potter, Ann Sebastian, Joan Marie Segreti, Carmen Shaw, Nancy Jo Walker, and Lilian Winer. They have sixty children, ranging in age from infancy to 20.

BOOKS BY MARIA MONTESSORI

The Absorbent Mind
The Discovery of the Child (This is the revised edition of the book which was given such especial approbation by Pope Benedict XV under its original title *The Advanced Montessori Method*)
Education for a New World
The Secret of Childhood
To Educate the Human Potential
The Formation of Man
What You Should Know About Your Child

PAMPHLETS BY MARIA MONTESSORI

The Child
The Child in the Church
Erdkinder and the Functions of the University
Reconstruction and Education
Peace and Education

ALSO

The Life and Works of Maria Montessori, by E. M. Standing
The Montessori Method, A Revolution in Education, by E. M. Standing
Learning How to Learn, by Nancy McCormick Rambush

www.ingramcontent.com/pod-product-compliance
Lightning Source LLC
LaVergne TN
LVHW091320080426
835510LV00007B/579